Colors

S0-AFD-175

Preschool/Kindergarten

Save time and energy planning thematic units with this comprehensive resource. We've searched the 1990–1998 issues of **The MAILBOX®** and **Teacher's Helper®** magazines to find the best ideas for you to use when teaching a thematic unit about colors. Included in this book are favorite units from the magazines, single ideas to extend a unit, and a variety of reproducible activities. Use these activities to develop your own complete unit or simply to add a colorful twist to your current lesson plans. You're sure to find everything you need for "color-rific" learning.

Editors:
Jayne M. Gammons
Michele M. Stoffel Menzel

Artist:
Teresa R. Davidson

Cover Artist:
Kimberly Richard

www.themailbox.com

Manufactured in the United States
10 9 8 7 6 5 4 3 2 1

Table Of Contents

Thematic Units

More Activities And Ideas

Reproducible Activities

Thematic Units...

from The MAILBOX® magazine

Splashes Of Red

Colorful ideas to help your little ones experience the color red!

Colorful Literature

Introduce your youngsters to the color red by reading red-related literature and dressing for the occasion! Wear articles of red clothing while reading aloud the book *Red Is Best* by Kathy Stinson (Firefly Books, Ltd.). After reading, ask each youngster to look around the classroom for items that are red. Then have your children sit in a circle to play a game similar to Hot Potato. Show them a red apple. As you play a musical recording, have each student in turn pass the apple to the child sitting next to him. Stop the music periodically, and have the child holding the apple stand up and point out an item that is red.

Need some other splashes of red? Try these colorful, red-related books:

> *Mary Wore Her Red Dress & Henry Wore His Green Sneakers* adapted and illustrated by Merle Peek (Clarion Books)
> *Is It Red? Is It Yellow? Is It Blue?* by Tana Hoban (Greenwillow Books)
> *Who Said Red?* written by Mary Serfozo and illustrated by Keiko Narahashi (Macmillan Children's Book Group)
> *Finding Red Finding Yellow* by Betsy Imershein (Check your library.)
> *The Red Poppy* by Irmgard Lucht and translated by Frank Jacoby-Nelson (Check your library.)

Red Day

Designate one day of the week to be Red Day. The day before, instruct youngsters to wear as many red articles of clothing as possible on Red Day. Then place a red stick-on dot on the back of each child's hand as a special reminder before he goes home. When this special day arrives, have your little ones discuss their red clothing with the rest of the class.

Circle Time

Little ones will love this "color-rific" circle-time idea. While learning about the color red, ask each youngster to bring a small, red item from home in a paper bag. During circle time, have each youngster bring his paper bag to the circle. Ask a student to volunteer to give the rest of the class clues about the object in his bag. Encourage the rest of the students to ask questions about the object; then have them try to guess what it is. Have the student volunteer reveal what's in his bag. Continue in this manner until each child has had a turn.

Really Red Fruit Salad

Stir up some colorful enthusiasm in your room by having youngsters create really red fruit salads. In advance, cut up pieces of red apples, cherries, watermelon, strawberries, and red grapes; then place each of the fruits in a different bowl. Place the bowls on a table. Provide each child with a red plastic spoon and a red cup. Encourage him to spoon the fruits of his choice from the bowls into his cup. Yum!

Centers With A Colorful Flair

- Try these quick-and-easy suggestions to help youngsters recognize the color red. Supply your math center with red poker chips, buttons, blocks, and other manipulatives. Have your little ones sort and classify the items by shape, size, and texture.

- Put a variety of red clothing in the dramatic play area, along with pictures or actual samples of red food items.

- Stock your art center with old magazines, scissors, red crayons, glue, and white construction paper. To use this center, have your students look through the magazines and cut out pictures of things that are red; then have them glue the pictures to the construction paper. A child may also choose to draw objects that are red. Now that's a red picture!

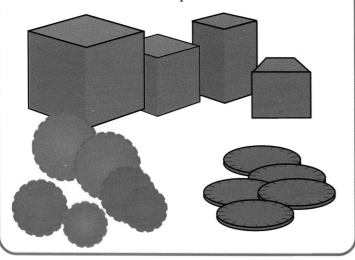

Moving Right Along

Select musical recordings carefully for this activity, and your youngsters will be color dancing in no time. Before starting the music, tape red crepe-paper streamers around each child's wrists. As you start the music, encourage your children to dance and move freely to the rhythm so that their streamers move expressively.

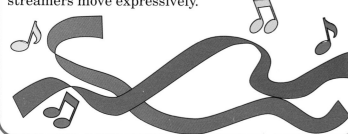

This looks like a flower. Katie

"Red-y" For Art?

- Your students will be caught red-handed with smiles of delight when making these creative collages. Supply each child with red craft items such as glitter, markers, glitter glue, sequins, ribbon, feathers, crayons, yarn, pompoms, and tissue paper. Have each child glue the craft items of his choice onto a large sheet of white construction paper. After the glue dries, allow time for each child to talk about his special collage.

- On another day, have each child place a dab of red paint inside a folded sheet of white construction paper. Refold the paper. Starting at the fold, have each child push the paint out toward the edges of his paper. Then have him open the folded paper to see his design. Have each child dictate a sentence about his design, as you write the sentence at the bottom of his paper.

- When your little ones do this red art activity, it will not only prove to be lots of fun, but your room will smell fresh and clean too. In advance, cover your tabletops with white bulletin-board paper. Squeeze a dab of shaving cream in front of each child; then add 1/4 teaspoon of red water-based paint or red powdered tempera paint to the shaving cream. Using his fingers, have each child mix the shaving cream and paint. Encourage each child to finger-paint with the red shaving cream, making the designs of his choice.

Judy Jones—Preschool; Get Ready, Set, Grow; Boca Raton, FL

Splashes Of Orange

Colorful ideas to help your little ones experience the color orange!

Color Of Autumn

Roll up your sleeves. Pass out the art smocks. It's time to be up to your elbows in orange paint! To introduce the color orange, scoop large dollops of red and yellow finger paint onto a clean table-top. Mist the tabletop with water. Encourage several students at a time to take turns smearing the two colors of paint to blend them. Monitor this process to stimulate discussions about what is happening to the paint and to mist the table whenever it becomes too dry. When youngsters have tired of finger-painting, press a giant, white, bulletin-board paper leaf cutout onto the table. Smooth it down; then carefully lift it up and place it where it can dry. Repeat this process several times, if desired, to "colorize" several giant leaf cutouts and to give each youngster an opportunity to mix red and yellow to get orange. Later post the leaves with student-dictated thoughts about things that become orange in autumn.

Orange Floats

A scoop of orange sherbet is the main ingredient in this irresistible drink. Lead into this activity by having students brainstorm foods and beverages that are orange. Ask students to tell what their favorite orange foods are. Slice or peel three or four oranges while the youngsters watch. As you discuss the color, smell, and taste of the fruit, have your preschoolers help you separate the oranges into sections. Put a scoop of orange sherbet in a small cup for each youngster. Then assist as each child pours some orange soda into the cup, garnishes the drink with a section of orange, and inserts a straw. While students are sipping their orange drinks, make it more of a festive occasion by singing the song in "Orange Sillies."

Orange Sillies

While students are sipping their orange floats (described above), lead them in singing a silly orange song. In the first four lines of the song, sing one phrase at a time, pausing for students to echo or repeat the phrase (indicated by italics), before singing the phrase on the next line.

Sippin'
(sung to the tune of "The Silliest Goat I Ever Saw")

The silliest girl (boy); *The silliest girl (boy)*
I ev-er saw; *I ev-er saw*
Was sip-pin' or-; *Was sip-pin' or-*
'Ange through a straw; *'Ange through a straw.*
The silliest girl (boy) I ev-er saw
Was sip-pin' o-range through a straw!

Outside Art

If your playground has a chain-link fence, you've got a great canvas for an orange weaving. To prepare for this activity, cut an orange fabric remnant (or an old sheet that has been dyed orange) into long, three-inch-wide strips. Also provide several similar strips of fabrics of different colors. In your collection, include assorted items that are orange. For example, you may include orange feathers, a string of plastic orange beads, some orange rickrack, or orange clothespins. Store the strips and other orange items in a laundry basket. Take your little ones outside and show them how to weave the strips in and out through the sections of the chain-link fence. Then let the creativity begin! Encourage students' participation in the weaving, but otherwise let the artwork evolve according to the preferences of the children. It's not necessary that the weaving resemble anything in particular. But when it's finally finished, you can step back and admire one thing for sure. That is really orange art!

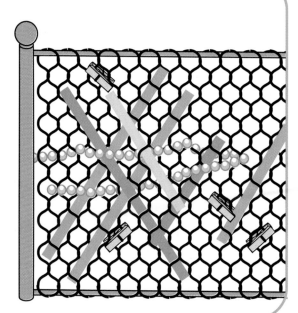

Orange Blossoms

Put out the word. Your class is on the lookout for orange papers and fabrics of all kinds. To get started, show students a few orange things that you have gathered. For example, you might have a remnant of orange cloth, sheets of several orange papers, and a woven orange produce bag. Explain that you are donating these things for a class project; then drop them into a collection bin labeled "orange." Encourage students to contribute to the orange box during the next few days.

When you have an adequate collection, cut the fabrics and papers into one-inch-wide strips. Provide each student with scissors, craft glue, and an 18-inch circle of white poster board. Have the youngster cut and glue strips of her choice to the circle to make a bright orange flower. Display each of the flowers along a classroom wall with paper leaves and stems of varying heights. What an amazing fall flower bed!

Orange Memories

Culminate your celebration of the color orange by setting aside a day to be Orange Day. Ask that on this day, each of the children wears something that is orange. (Have on hand a box of orange accessories—such as badges, hats, and shoestrings—for youngsters who forget about Orange Day.) Once everyone is all decked out in orange, invite them to look in a full-length mirror, then draw their likenesses on art paper. Help each student complete a fill-in-the-blank sentence about the orange clothing he is wearing. Then use masking tape to bind the artwork into a booklet with an orange-embellished cover.

M. Lynne Sypher, Brook Avenue School, Bay Shore, NY

Splashes Of Yellow

Colorful ideas to help your little ones experience the color yellow!

Yellow, Yellow, Everywhere!

Brainstorm a list of yellow things with your youngsters. Then sing this bright and cheery song to the tune of "Twinkle, Twinkle, Little Star."

Yellow, yellow, bright and fair;
Yellow, yellow, everywhere.
Lemonade and apples, too;
Golden yellow hair on you.
Yellow, yellow, bright and fair;
Yellow, yellow, everywhere.

Tracy Lynn Troup—Pre-K

When Life Gives You Lemons

Make lemon prints and lemonade! In advance cut a quantity of lemons in half lengthwise. Set several of the lemon halves aside to dry slightly. Store the remaining halves in a refrigerator. Then, in an art center, place the lemon halves, white construction paper, newspaper, and a pan of yellow tempera paint. Encourage each child to dip a lemon half in the paint, press it onto the newspaper, and then press it onto a sheet of construction paper. Have him continue in this manner until he has several prints on his paper. As a nifty follow-up activity, make lemonade with the leftover lemons!

Tracy Lynn Troup—Pre-K

Tasty Graphing

Stir up some excitement in your room when graphing youngsters' favorite yellow foods. Using yellow paper, create a graph with the name and picture of each yellow food that will be tasted. Place a variety of yellow foods—such as bananas, cheese, corn, scrambled eggs, macaroni and cheese, and corn bread—on a table. Provide each child with a yellow plate and a plastic spoon. Have each child place a portion of each food on his plate, and encourage him to taste each food. Supply each child with a personalized, yellow happy-face cutout. Have each student indicate his favorite yellow food by placing his happy face in the appropriate place on the graph. Ask questions such as "How many children like cheese the best?" and "Do more people like bananas or cheese?"

Tracy Lynn Troup—Pre-K
Family Day Care/Preschool
Lebanon, PA

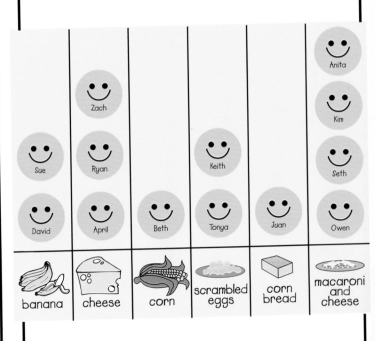

Yellow Mellow Butter

Read aloud *Brown Cow, Green Grass, Yellow Mellow Sun* by Ellen Jackson (Hyperion Books for Children). Spread out the fun of the story by having your youngsters make yellow mellow butter. To make butter, provide each child with a small, plastic jar half filled with room-temperature whipping cream. Secure the lid on each jar. Have each child shake, shake, shake, until the cream is yellow mellow butter. Provide each child with a plastic knife and a slice of bread, and have him spread some of his homemade butter atop the bread. Yum!

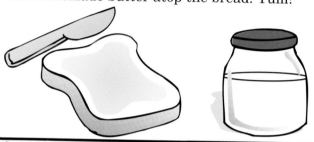

Yellow, Yellow, Friendly Fellow

Keep a small, round, yellow pillow in a prominent place for your students to hold when they are feeling gloomy. When a child needs a little extra attention, encourage him to hold the yellow, yellow, friendly fellow pillow. Remind the class to give that student some tender loving care for the day.

Kathy Mulvihill—Four-Year-Olds
Wee Care Preschool
Allendale, MI

You Are My Sunshine

These suns will make you happy when skies are gray. Provide each child with a tagboard circle cutout and yellow tissue-paper pieces. Have each student glue the tissue paper onto the tagboard so that the pieces overlap to cover the circle. Then have each youngster drizzle yellow or gold glitter glue atop the tissue paper. When the glue is dry, glue several yellow streamers to the edge of the circle to resemble a sun. Encourage each of your little ones to hold his sun cutout above his head while singing "You Are My Sunshine" or while listening to Raffi's "One Light, One Sun."

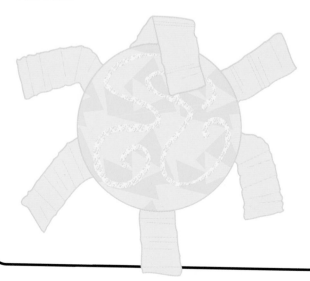

The Yellow Pages

Need a unique art technique? Look in the yellow pages! Reuse old telephone books by removing the yellow pages. Encourage youngsters to tear or cut the pages, then glue them to black construction paper. You'll be able to call these collages one-of-a-kind!

Literature Links

Yellow Ball
Written & Illustrated by Molly Bang
(Check your library.)

Little Blue And Little Yellow
Written & Illustrated by Leo Lionni
Published by Mulberry Books

Splashes Of Green

Colorful ideas to help your little ones experience the color green!

Green From Tip To Tail

Watch out! With this art project, you'll have a slithery, sneaky snake that changes colors. To make a giant snake, you'll need a large piece of finger-painting paper for each child. Tape the papers together, end to end, to create one long strip. Trim along the top and bottom of the strip in a wavy manner, so that it resembles a snake. Using permanent markers, create features and attach a red construction-paper tongue. Spread the snake shape out in a long, uncarpeted hallway or on a long strip of plastic. On each child's section of paper, drop a dollop of blue and yellow finger paint. Then invite several children at a time to put on art smocks and finger-paint their sections of the paper snake. When all sections have been painted and have dried, mount the snake on the wall.

It's A Jungle In There!

Surround your youngsters with the color green by transforming your classroom into a growing green room. Set the mood by draping your cabinets, shelves, and windows with artificial greenery. During a group time, ask your little ones to brainstorm a list of things that can be green. Write each child's suggestion on a large, light green paper leaf shape. Then ask each child to illustrate his suggestion on his leaf with crayons or paints. Mount the illustrated leaf shapes onto slightly larger, dark green paper leaf shapes. Attach each leaf to a green, crepe-paper streamer and suspend it from the ceiling. Now you're growing wild with green!

Grapes are green. Samuel

Dip And Nibble

By now your youngsters have been surrounded with green for viewing and have been up to their elbows in green for touching. What's next in experiencing the color green? Tasting, of course! On your next trip to the grocery store, shop for an assortment of green vegetables such as broccoli, celery, green peppers, zucchini, and cucumbers. (Or ask parents to contribute these vegetables.) Cut the green veggies into portions just right for preschoolers to dip and nibble on. (Save some of the vegetables for "Tossed-Salad Art.") Add green food coloring to ranch dressing; then pour the dressing into small cups or bowls. Provide each child with a cup of the dressing for dipping the vegetables of his choice.

Tossed-Salad Art

Using the green vegetables suggested in "Dip And Nibble," have students make vegetable prints. In an art center, place the cut vegetables and a pie tin of green paint. Provide each child in the center with a white paper plate. Encourage her to dip one of the vegetables in the paint and press it onto the plate. Have her repeat this process using the various vegetables. To create a display, cover a table with a green paper tablecloth. Tape the dry vegetable prints to the tablecloth along with a sign titled "Tossed-Salad Art."

adapted from an idea by
 Suzanne Costner
Maryville, TN

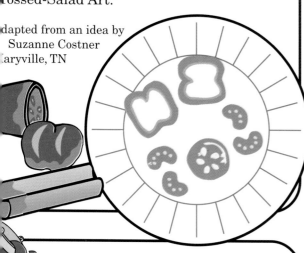

Green Giggles And Jiggles

Make a batch of lime-flavored Jell-O® Jigglers® gelatin snacks, and you are sure to hear lots of giggles from your little ones. To make the gelatin snacks, follow the directions on a package of lime-flavored Jell-O® brand gelatin. Then provide youngsters with cookie cutters in the shapes of trees, dinosaurs, and other things that can be green. Assist each child in using the cutter of his choice to cut out a gelatin snack. If desired, provide whipped topping that has been tinted green and green sprinkles for topping the treats. Watch them wiggle! See them jiggle!

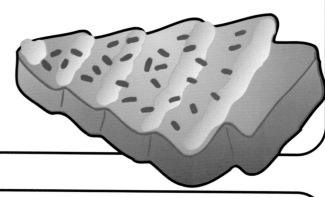

The Grass Is Greener

The ground might be covered with snow outside, but in your class the grass is green and growing. Collect a class supply of half-pint milk cartons. Clean the cartons and cut off their tops. Provide each child with a strip of paper cut to match the height of the carton and long enough to wrap around it. Have each child paint his strip green. While the paint is wet, have him sprinkle the strip with green glitter. When it's dry, tape or glue the strip around a carton. Assist each child in filling his carton with soil. Have him gently press a spoonful of birdseed into the dirt. Place the cartons by a window and watch the green grass grow.

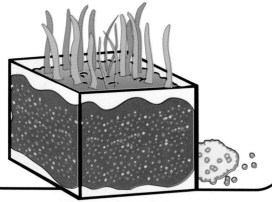

"It's Not Easy Being Green"

Bring your celebration of the color green to a close by listening to everyone's favorite frog sing "Bein' Green." A recording of the song can be found on *Sesame Street Platinum: All-Time Favorites* (Sony/Wonder). If possible, manipulate a frog puppet while playing the song.

Splashes Of Blue

Colorful ideas to help your little ones experience the color blue!

Blueberries For You

Introduce the color blue with this "berry" nice idea. On a designated day, ask youngsters to wear as many articles of blue clothing as possible. Ask them to bring a toy bear to school on the same day. Upon students' arrival, seat them in a group and read aloud *Blueberries For Sal* by Robert McCloskey (Puffin Books). Explain that since everyone has a bear, it must be time for berry picking. All you need are berry buckets.

To make a bucket for each child, fold down several inches of a closed, white paper bag. Cut a half-circle shape through all thicknesses; then unfold and open the bag. Program each bag with the phrase "Blueberry Bucket." Have each child paint a green bush on his bag. Next have him dip a pencil eraser in blue paint, then press it onto the bag to resemble blueberries. While the students are decorating their blueberry buckets, ask an adult volunteer to hide blueberry snacks, such as blueberries in plastic bags that have been tied with blue ribbons, blueberry cereal bars, blueberry muffins, or blueberry tarts. When the paint dries, let the hunting begin! Have each child hold his blueberry bucket and his bear, and hunt for a blueberry snack. Enjoy another reading of *Blueberries For Sal* while your little ones snack, snack, snack!

Linda Ludlow
Bethesda Christian Schools
Brownsburg, IN

Blueberry Bucket

The Deep Blue Sea

Give your water table a feel of the deep blue sea with these exciting additions. Add several drops of blue food coloring to the water. Then add plastic or sponge undersea creatures such as sea horses, starfish, fish, jelly-fish, crabs, and lobsters. Play a recording of ocean sounds while little ones dive into some serious play.

Dalia Behr—Preschool
The Little Dolphin School
Ozone Park, NY

Blue Jigglers®

Mixing up these colorful treats in your classroom will no doubt cure the blues. Prepare a pan of blue Jell-O® Jigglers® following the package directions. Then cut the gelatin into small squares to make individual Jigglers. Provide each child with several Jiggle on a blue paper plate; then allow you little ones to sample these yummy treats while listening to Sesame Street's Grover sing "I Am Blue."

Dalia Behr—Preschool

Blue-Jean Collage

It's all in the jeans—at least in this crafty collage. Provide each child with a blue construction-paper pant shape and scraps of old denim blue jeans. Have each student glue the denim scraps to the pant shape in the design of his choice. Now that's some casual creativity!

Theresa Anderson—Two- And Three-Year-Olds
Children's World Learning Center
Rochester, MN

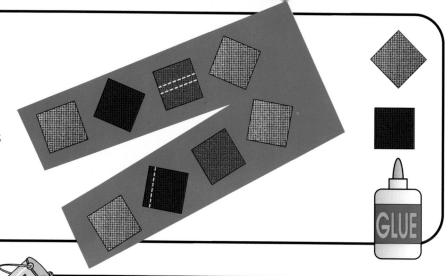

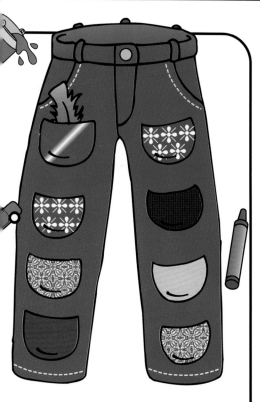

Pockets Full Of Blue

This fun-filled activity will be pockets full of fun. On a pair of old blue jeans, sew or hot-glue blue fabric to create pockets. Place a supply of different-colored small objects in a basket, making certain that there are enough blue objects for each pocket on the jeans. Place the jeans and the basket in a center. To use this center, a child chooses an object from the basket and identifies the color of the object. If the object is blue, he places it in one of the pockets on the pair of jeans. If the object is a different color, he places it back in the basket.

Deborah Ladd
Mustang, OK

I Spy Something Blue

All eyes are searching for something blue with this investigative idea. Provide each child with a cardboard tube that has been painted blue. Have each youngster hold his tube to his eye to represent a spyglass and look for blue objects around the classroom. Have a student volunteer name a blue object that he spies. Continue in this manner until each child has had a turn. Then take youngsters outside to search for other blue items. I spy a blue sky!

Kathy Mulvihill—Four-Year-Olds, Wee Care Preschool, Allendale, MI

A Blue Suncatcher

Put those old, blue crayons to good use by making colorful suncatchers. To make a suncatcher, grate various shades of blue crayons. Provide each child with two 3 1/2" squares of waxed paper. Have her sprinkle some of the crayon shavings on one piece of the waxed paper. Have her place the other waxed-paper square on top of the shavings. Place both sheets of paper on a towel; then place a cloth over the waxed paper. Gently press a warm iron atop the cloth until the crayon shavings in the center of the waxed paper have melted. When the paper has cooled, have each child glue four craft sticks over the edges of the paper square to make a frame. Glue a piece of blue yarn to the back to suspend the suncatcher. Now that's "blue-tiful"!

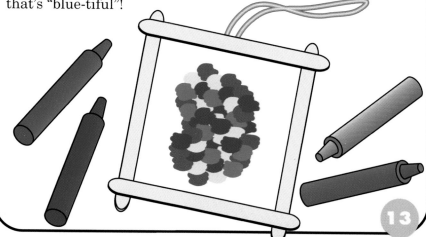

13

Splashes Of Purple

Colorful ideas to help your little ones experience the color purple!

Welcome To Purpleville

Introduce your youngsters to the color purple by transforming your classroom into Purpleville. Before students arrive, embellish your classroom cabinets, windows, and shelves with purple streamers, curling ribbon, and inflated balloons. Cover each table or desk with purple bulletin-board paper. Place a vase filled with artificial purple flowers and a purple paper plate with purple grapes on each desk or table. On the front of your classroom door, tape a sign that reads "Welcome To Purpleville." As your little ones enter, lead them in singing the following song. Have youngsters substitute a different action each time the verse is sung.

The Land Of Purpleville

(sung to the tune of "Here We Go Round The Mulberry Bush")

In the land of Purpleville,
The children there wear purple still.
They love to dance and they love to sing,
And they love to [clap their hands].

Jean Harrison
Palm Bay, FL

Purple Pizzazz

These purple foods have lots of pizzazz. Begin by having your youngsters brainstorm purple foods. Have a few food items such as an eggplant, purple grapes, beets, and red cabbage on hand to display and discuss. After the discussion, ask youngsters to name beverages that are purple. Then show them a bottle of grape soda. For each child, put a scoop of vanilla ice cream in a purple cup. Then assist as each child pours some grape soda into the cup and garnishes the ice cream with purple cake sprinkles. "Purple-licious!"

Color Me A Cookie

Try this sweet idea for some colorful fun. Bake sugar cookies from refrigerated dough according to the package directions. When the cookies have cooled, provide each group of children with cookies, plastic knives, and a small bowl of purple icing (use icing in a tube or add purple concentrated paste to vanilla icing). Encourage each child to cover his cookie with the purple icing. Then have each child top off his cookie with a dab of grape jelly, if desired, and enjoy it!

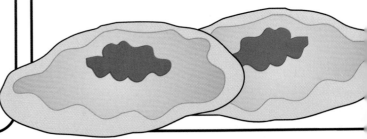

A Royal Show-And-Tell

Your students will feel like kings and queens with this royal idea. In advance paint a medium-size box and its lid purple. When the paint is dry, stock a center with the box, scissors, glue, and purple craft items such as yarn, ribbon, pom-poms, fake jewels, sequins, lace, feathers, felt pieces, and tissue-paper pieces. Then let the decorating begin! Encourage youngsters to embellish the box with the provided items so that it resembles a royal treasure chest.

Later designate one day to be Royal Show-And-Tell Day. On the day before, encourage each child to wear something that is purple and to bring in a purple object from home. As each child enters the classroom on this special day, have him place his purple object in the decorated treasure chest. During show-and-tell, seat your youngsters in a circle on the floor and place the chest in the middle of the circle. In turn, crown each child with a purple construction-paper crown and place a piece of purple cloth around his shoulders to represent a royal cloak. Then have each child describe his purple object without naming it. Have the rest of the class try to guess what the object is before it is revealed.

Jean Harrison
Palm Bay, FL

Ready To Make Purple?

Your little artists will love letting their creative juices flow with this fun idea. On a clean table in front of each child, place dabs of red and blue washable paint. Ask him what he thinks will happen when the two colors are mixed. Using his hands, have each student mix the two colors together. Encourage each child to use his fingers to make the design of his choice in the paint. When each child is satisfied with his creation, gently place a sheet of white construction paper atop his design. Rub your hand lightly over the entire paper. Lift the paper and let the paint dry.

After having each of your youngsters share their prints, have them sing the following song, substituting a different action each time the verse is sung:

If You Like The Color Purple
(sung to the tune of "If You're Happy And You Know It")

If you like the color purple, [clap your hands].
   Clap twice.
If you like the color purple, [clap your hands].
   Clap twice.
You can make the color true,
By mixing red and blue;
If you like the color purple, [clap your hands].
   Clap twice.

Jean Harrison

How Now, Purple Cow?

Here's a "moo-velous" idea for reviewing the color purple. In advance, use a purple marker or chalk to copy Gelette Burgess's "The Purple Cow" (from memory or a poetry book such as *Favorite Poems Old And New* edited by Helen Ferris) on a chalkboard or piece of chart paper. Ask your students if they have ever seen a purple cow. Graph the results and discuss what the graph reveals. Read the poem aloud; then let students volunteer to share their reactions to the poem. Read the poem several more times, having youngsters join in as they are able. Then give each child a cow-shaped cutout and have him decorate it using art supplies such as purple construction-paper scraps, crayons, glitter, tissue-paper pieces, and buttons.

MOUSE PAINT

Written & Illustrated by Ellen Stoll Walsh
Published by Harcourt Brace & Company

As this cat-and-mouse tale unfolds, a trio of rambunctious rodents splashes and dances its way through red, yellow, and blue paint. Read aloud *Mouse Paint;* then follow up the story with these color-mixing lessons that are full of whiskers and whimsy. *Mouse Paint* is available in hardback, paperback, as a board book, and as a big book from Harcourt Brace & Company: 1-800-543-1918.

ideas by Lisa Leonardi

Mouse Hide-And-Seek

To prepare for a scampering round of mouse hide-and-seek, cut a classroom supply of mouse shapes from white construction paper (pattern on page 18). Using tape or Sticky-Tac, hide the cutouts against the white backgrounds of your room—such as white walls or bulletin boards. Ask each of your little ones to pretend he is the cat in the story and encourage him to prowl around your room in search of a mouse. When he finds one, have him remove the adhesive and write his name on one side with crayon. Later invite each child to visit your art center to give his mouse a dip (see "Taking A Dip").

Taking A Dip

If your little ones are still pretending to be cats, have them lie down to take a nap like the cat in the book. Remind them that in the story, when the cat went to sleep, the mice climbed into the mouse paint. In an art center, fill each of three jars with watered-down red, yellow, or blue paint. Then, as the group rests, invite one child at a time to tiptoe over to your art center with his mouse cutout. Encourage him to dip his mouse in the jar of his choice, then pat it dry with a paper towel. Next encourage the child to dip the mouse into one of the two remaining colors. Repeat the drying process. When each child has had an opportunity to take his mouse for a dip, awaken the group from their catnap and gather them together. Discuss the results of each mouse's mischief.

Ellen Stoll Walsh

The Pitter-Patter Of Painted Feet

Your youngsters are guaranteed to jump feetfirst into this activity that encourages them to pretend to be mice instead of cats. To prepare for this slightly messy mouse activity, spread a protective covering over the floor near your painting area. Fill a tub with warm, soapy water and set some old towels nearby. Fill three different paint pots with red, yellow, and blue paint. Fill three different pie pans with the same colors. Select some lively music to back up the fun.

As a group, discuss the pages that show each paint-covered mouse dancing in a puddle. Ask each child to remove her shoes and socks, roll up her pants, and pretend to be a mouse. Direct her to use a brush to paint a red, yellow, or blue puddle on a large piece of paper. Next have her step in the pie pan containing one of the two remaining colors. As music plays, have her dance with painted feet on her paper, swirling the colors together to create a secondary color. When she is finished, have her wash and dry her feet. Now that's a masterpiece that's quite a "feet!"

Sugar And Spice And Everything Mice!

These colorful treats are a "mouse-ful!" Bake or purchase a classroom quantity of sugar cookies. Give each child a cookie on a sheet of waxed paper. Drop a spoonful of white icing onto his sheet. Have him decide which secondary color he would like his mouse to be. If he's not sure which two colors of food coloring to add to his icing, let him check the pages of *Mouse Paint*. Once he has added several drops of each color to his icing, have him blend the colors with a craft stick, then spread the icing on his cookie. Finally have him add raisin eyes and a nose, pretzel-stick whiskers, and gumdrop ears. Your little "mouseketeers" won't be able to resist these tasty mouse morsels!

A Collection Of Colors

Culminate your activities as the mice did at the end of the story—by painting a mural. Enlarge the mouse pattern on page 18 onto the bottom corner of a length of white bulletin-board paper. Visually divide the paper into thirds. Using the appropriate colors of markers, label each third *red + yellow = orange, blue + yellow = green,* or *red + blue = purple.* Provide your little ones with red, yellow, and blue paint and paintbrushes. Encourage them to paint the mural, using the primary colors of paint to create secondary colors. Be sure to leave the mouse white...just in case the cat comes back!

Mouse Parents

Encourage parents to join in the "color-ific" fun! Duplicate a copy of the parent note on page 18 for each child. Encourage youngsters to color the mice on the notes before sending them home.

Barry Slate

Mouse Pattern

Use with "Mouse Hide-And-Seek" and "Taking A Dip" on page 16 and "A Collection Of Colors" on page 17.

©The Education Center, Inc. • *Colors* • Preschool/Kindergarten • TEC3172

Parent Note

Use with "Mouse Parents" on page 17.

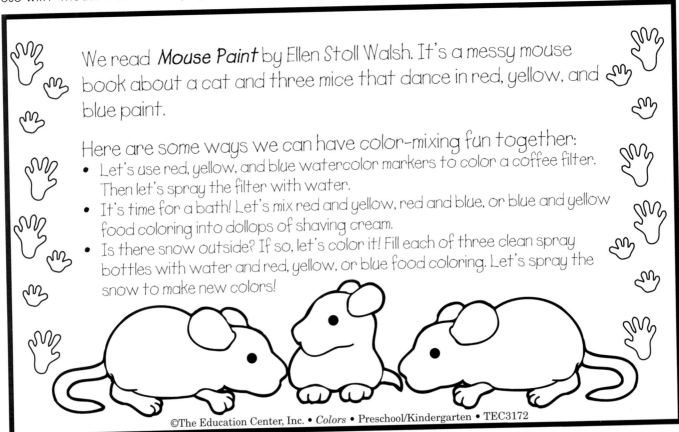

We read **Mouse Paint** by Ellen Stoll Walsh. It's a messy mouse book about a cat and three mice that dance in red, yellow, and blue paint.

Here are some ways we can have color-mixing fun together:
- Let's use red, yellow, and blue watercolor markers to color a coffee filter. Then let's spray the filter with water.
- It's time for a bath! Let's mix red and yellow, red and blue, or blue and yellow food coloring into dollops of shaving cream.
- Is there snow outside? If so, let's color it! Fill each of three clean spray bottles with water and red, yellow, or blue food coloring. Let's spray the snow to make new colors!

©The Education Center, Inc. • *Colors* • Preschool/Kindergarten • TEC3172

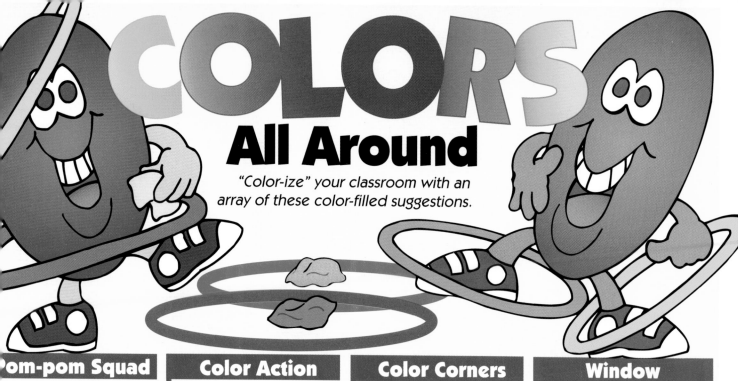

COLORS
All Around

"Color-ize" your classroom with an array of these color-filled suggestions.

Pom-pom Squad

When you keep a large supply of different-colored pom-poms on hand, you've got the makings for a myriad of color activities that suit many different classroom themes. For example, scatter all of the pom-poms around your room. Have one group of children collect and place all of the red pom-poms in a pie pan to resemble a cherry pie. Ask additional groups of children to collect and place the green ones in a pot (peas), the brown ones in a basket (nuts), the white ones in a pile (snow), and so on.

You can also use the scattered pom-poms in exciting "races." Assign a different color to each of several teams. At your signal, have the teams quickly gather the appropriate pom-poms and place them in their respective containers.

Tara Schlotter—Preschool
Faith Christian Child Care
Washington, IL

Color Action

For more color fun, combine your color study with a bevy of motor skills. Arrange different colors of Hula-Hoops® on a floor or outdoors. Give each child a beanbag. Position children randomly around the hoops. Have each child follow your color-related directions such as "If you have brown hair, toss your beanbag into a purple hoop"; "Put your beanbag on your head, step into a hoop, and name that color"; and "If you are wearing pink, jump into a pink hoop; then toss your beanbag into a yellow hoop."

At another time, provide each pair or small group of children with a different-colored balloon. Have youngsters tap the balloons in the air, trying not to let the balloons fall to the ground. After several minutes, call out a direction such as "Red, tap with yellow!" Then have the red and yellow groups tap their balloons back and forth to each other.

Christine A. Wilber
Preschool Hearing Impaired
San Marino School
Buena Park, CA

Color Corners

Here's a colorful twist on the traditional Four Corners game. Tape a different color of construction paper in each of the corners of your classroom. Place a stack of color cards, facedown, in a central location. (You can use manufactured cards or make your own by gluing different colors of construction paper onto white construction-paper cards.) Have each child walk to any corner of the room that he chooses. Then turn over the top color card. After youngsters name the color on the card, each child who is standing in that particular color's corner takes his seat. Continue playing in the same manner—having students move to different corners before each card is drawn—until only one child is left standing. Then begin round two!

Catherine L. Pesa
Pre-K/K Hearing Impaired
Paul C. Bunn School
Youngstown, OH

Window Wonders

These mock stained-glass windows make a dazzling display on a sunny day. Give each child a square of clear adhesive covering. Have him arrange and press different colors of small tissue-paper shapes onto the sticky side of the covering. When each child is done, you can adhere his work directly onto a glass window or seal it with another identically sized piece of adhesive covering before taping it to your classroom window.

Shelley L. Hansen—Preschool
WSU Child Development Center
Wichita, KS

What Do You Mean, Green?

Read aloud Leo Lionni's warm and appealing *Little Blue And Little Yellow* (published by Mulberry Books). After discussing the story, ask each child if she thinks yellow mixed with blue really makes green. Then give each child a sheet of white construction paper that has been folded in equal thirds. As you demonstrate—going from left to right—have each child draw a "+" on the first fold and an "=" on the second fold. After explaining the meaning of the symbols, have each child use a paintbrush to paint a yellow shape in the first section. Using a different brush, have her paint a blue shape in the second section. Then have each child use both brushes to paint one shape in the last section. What do they think?

Andrea Esposito—Preschool
VA/YMCA Day Care
Brooklyn, NY

Cool Colors

Dip into some more color exploring with ice cubes! Read a book featuring primary and secondary colors, such as Monique Felix's adorable, wordless picture book, *The Colors* (published by Creative Education). After reading and discussing the book, fill three ice-cube trays with water. Using food coloring, color the water in the trays to result in a tray each of red, blue, and yellow; then freeze the trays. Give each small group of children three clear plastic cups; a bowl with several of each color of ice cubes; and red, blue, and yellow stickers. Have youngsters place different combinations of two ice-cube colors in each of the cups. Instruct them to place the corresponding stickers on the outside of each cup so they will know what the original cube colors were. With the extra ice cubes, have children "paint" on white construction paper by sliding the ice cubes on the paper. When the ice cubes in the cups have melted, come back to see the results!

Cara Schlotter—Preschool
Faith Christian Child Care, Washington, IL

Lauren Wiethorn—Gr. K
Ayer Elementary School, Cincinnati, OH

Colorful Chameleons

A chameleon makes a perfect topic of conversation when you're studying colors. Read aloud *The Mixed-Up Chameleon* by Eric Carle (published by HarperTrophy) or *Color Of His Own* by Leo Lionni (published by Pantheon Books). After discussing the story, give each child a large construction-paper chameleon. With the help of another adult, spoon dabs of two different primary colors onto each chameleon, being sure that the two colors do not touch each other. Review the mixed-up chameleon character in the book; then tell youngsters that their chameleons are mixed-up too—they can't decide which colors to be. Then have youngsters use paintbrushes to combine the colors. There—that's just what I wanted to be!

Karen Attanasio—Preschool
Back Mountain Memorial Library
Dallas, PA

My Mouse Paint Book by Jeremy

Pam Crane

Mouse-Paint Booklet

After sharing *Mouse Paint* by Ellen Stoll Walsh (published by Harcourt Brace Jovanovich), children will be eager to make their own Mouse-Paint booklets. Duplicate three copies of the middle page booklet pattern (page 23). Program each mouse on these pages as indicated below. Then, for each child, duplicate each programmed page and the title and back booklet pages (pages 23–24) on construction paper. Give each child a set of booklet pages. Have a copy or two of *Mouse Paint* available for youngsters' reference. Direct each child to color or paint the mice on the middle pages according to the color words. Then have them color or paint the mouse on the bottom of each page accordingly and write or dictate the color word. After coloring/painting and completing the title and back booklet pages, have each child staple the pages together. Encourage each child to take his booklet home and read and/or retell the story to his family members.

Lauren Wiethorn—Gr. K
Ayer Elementary School
Cincinnati, OH

red + blue

yellow + red

blue + yellow

blue + yellow = green

Color Outing

Explore additional uses of color by taking a trip to a local art museum. Give each child a square of colored construction paper. Have each child look for that particular color as you tour the museum. After a few minutes, have each child exchange his color square with a classmate who has a different-colored square. Continue touring the museum in the same manner. Have youngsters switch color squares every once in a while so that each child is encouraged to look for every color.

Shelley L. Hansen—Preschool
WSU Child Development Center
Wichita, KS

Color Cooperation

Making this cooperative mural is another terrific follow-up activity for a book such as *Mouse Paint*. To prepare, make job tickets by cutting out 18 construction-paper ticket shapes. (If you have more or fewer than 18 children in your class, adjust the colors and jobs accordingly.) Color code three tickets each for red, yellow, blue, orange, green, and purple. In each color set, label each ticket with one symbol as follows: (1) "looking," (2) "cutting," and (3) "gluing." Place a long sheet of bulletin-board paper on a flat surface along with colorful magazines, scissors, and glue. Give each child a ticket; then direct children to group themselves according to their color tickets. Have each child refer to his ticket and, accordingly, look for magazine pictures in that particular color, cut out the pictures, or glue them to the paper. Display the finished mural within each child's reach; then have youngsters use black construction-paper strips and reusable adhesive to connect secondary colors to the primary colors that make them.

Barb Spero—Grade K, Memorial School
Paramus, NJ

Jodie

Dancing Rainbow

When you combine a little gross-motor activity with these projects, the results are beautiful! Make a rainbow by gluing six lengths of different-colored crepe-paper streamers to one side edge of a paper plate. (If your class is studying rainbows, glue the streamers in the correct order [from top to bottom]: red, orange, yellow, green, blue, and violet.) After personalizing each plate, play some beautiful music while youngsters dance with their rainbows. Or go outdoors and let children experiment with their rainbows, physical movements, and the wind.

Ann Scalley—Pre/K, Wellfleet Preschool
Wellfleet, MA

Rainbow Booklet

These pretty rainbow booklets employ fine-motor skills as well as reinforcing color and color-word recognition. For each child, duplicate the rainbow booklet pages (pages 25–28) on white construction paper. On each booklet page indicating a color, have each child color that section of the rainbow in the appropriate color, then trace the color word on that page. Assist each child in cutting along the bold lines on each of his booklet pages. Then challenge each child to arrange his booklet pages in order. Staple the pages together along the left edge. Read the booklets together during a group reading time. Youngsters will be proud to share these impressive booklets with their families.

Anita Ortiz
Red Sandstone Elementary
Vail, CO

Pretty rainbow way up high,
What are your colors in the sky?

green

red

Color Books

A Color Sampler
Written by Kathleen Westray
Published by Ticknor & Fields

Color Zoo
Written & Illustrated by Lois Ehlert
Published by J. B. Lippincott

Going Up!: A Color Counting Book
Written & Illustrated by Peter Sis
(Check your library.)

Of Colors And Things
Written & Illustrated by Tana Hoban
Published by Greenwillow Books

Samuel Todd's Book Of Great Colors
Written & Illustrated by E. L. Konigsburg
Published by Aladdin Paperbacks

The Purple Coat
Written by Amy Hest
Illustrated by Amy Schwartz
Published by Four Winds Press

Who Said Red?
Written by Mary Serfozo
Illustrated by Keiko Narahashi
Published by Aladdin Books

Oh, Were They Ever Happy!
Written & Illustrated by Peter Spier
(Check your library.)

Use these pages with "Mouse-Paint Booklet" on page 21.

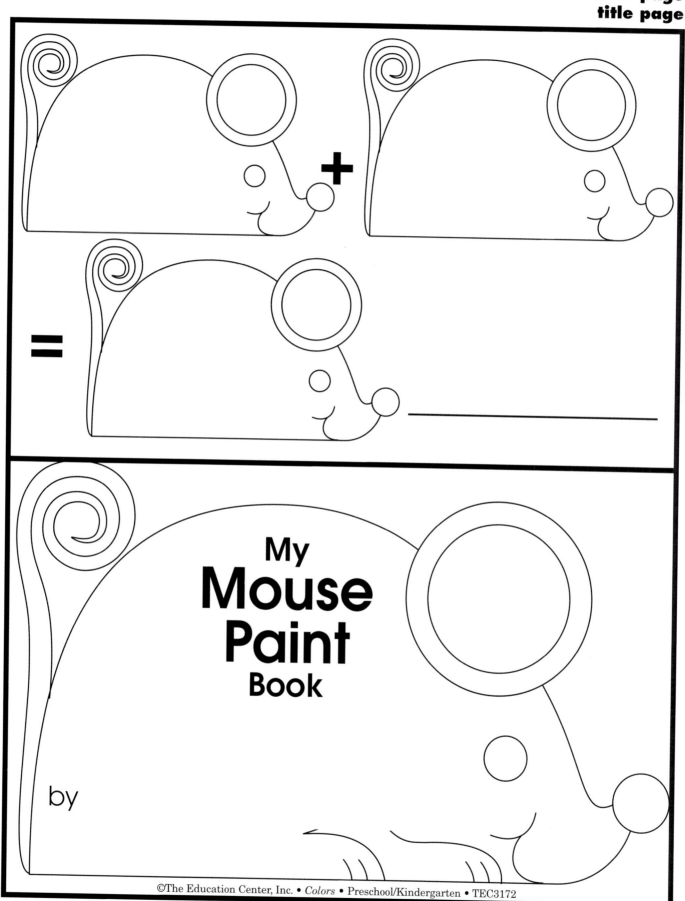

My
Mouse
Paint
Book

by

My favorite mouse looks like this.

red

purple

green

orange

yellow

blue

_____

knows all of
these
colors!

©The Education Center, Inc. • *Colors* • Preschool/Kindergarten • TEC3172

Note To The Teacher: Duplicate; then personalize the award for each child. Have children color the awards before taking them home.

Pretty rainbow way up high,
What are your colors in the sky?

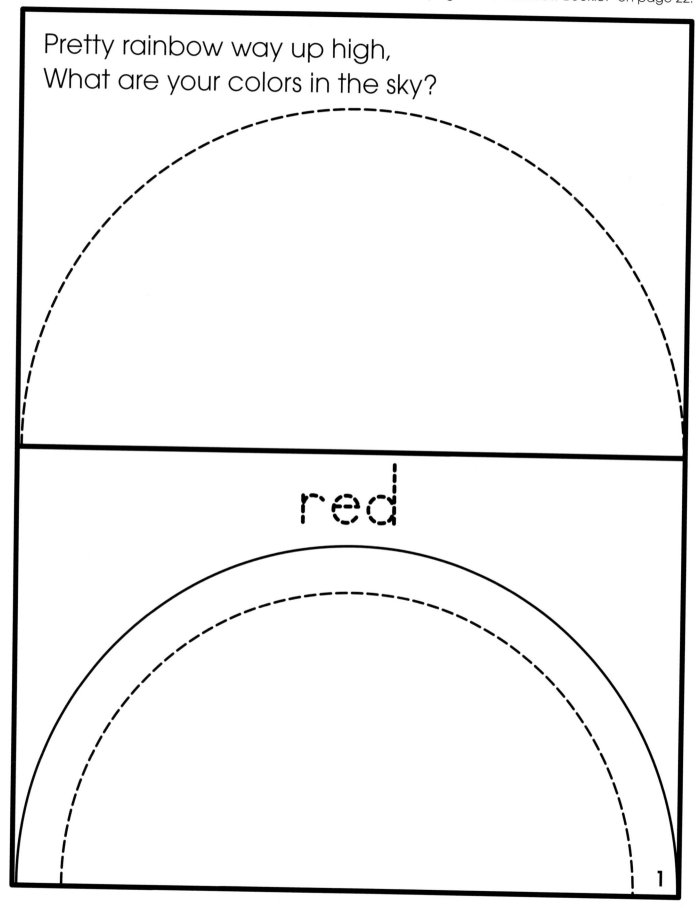

red

1

Rainbow Booklet Pages

Use these pages with "Rainbow Booklet" on page 22.

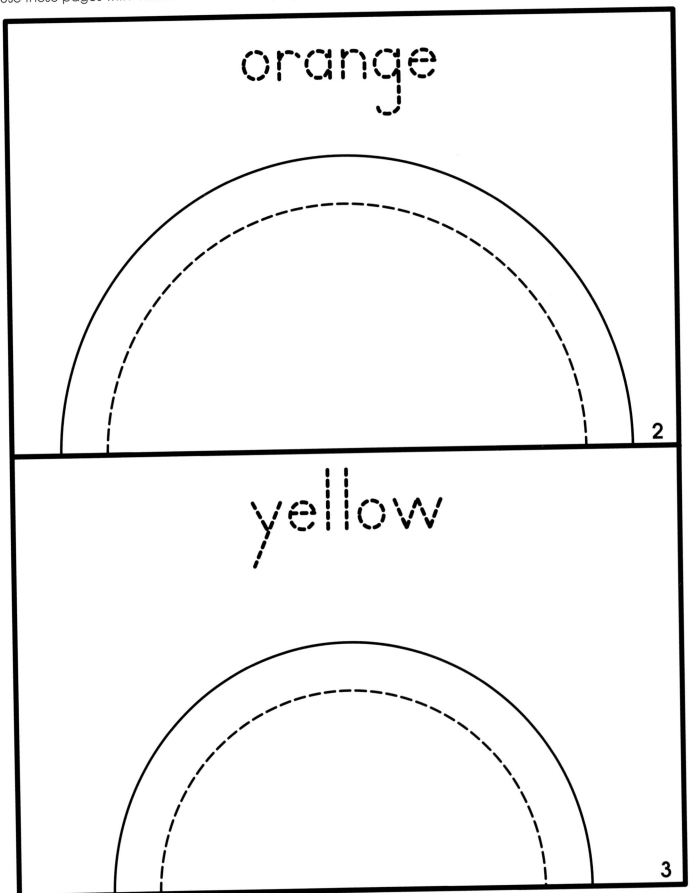

orange

2

yellow

3

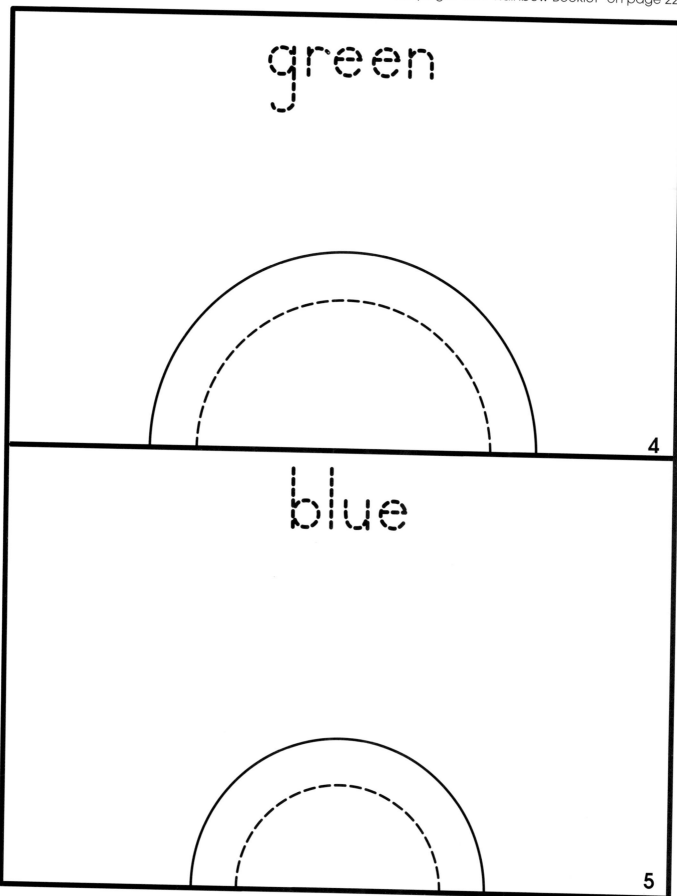

green

4

blue

5

Rainbow Booklet Pages

Use these pages with "Rainbow Booklet" on page 22.

purple

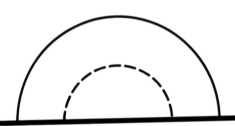

6

All these colors that I know
Live up in the rainbow!

7

"Painted" Marshmallows

As an extension of *Mouse Paint* by Ellen Stohl, youngsters can explore the wonder of colors with painted marshmallows. To make a painted marshmallow, squeeze a few drops of red, yellow, or blue food coloring onto a piece of waxed paper; then squeeze a few drops of a second primary color close to, but not touching, the first color. Using a large marshmallow, swirl the two colors together to create a secondary color. What a colorful and tasty treat!

Sara Davis—Gr. K
Wiley Post School
Putnam City, OK

Dot-To-Dot

Little ones can hop dot-to-dot with this sequential motor-skill game. Cut 6-inch dots from different colors of Con-Tact® covering. Secure the circles to the floor in the pattern of five dots on a die. When you need an instant activity, challenge a child to hop on the dots according to a directed oral sequence of colors. For example, you might say, "Hop on a blue dot, a red dot, then a yellow dot" or "Hop on a yellow dot three times, then a green dot three times." Modify your directions to match individual students' needs and abilities. Or offer to let a child give you directions. Happy hopping!

Joyce Montag—Preschool
Slippery Rock Park
Slippery Rock, PA

Color Wizardry

Put a touch of color-mixing magic into your classroom with these manipulative bags. To prepare a bag, squirt a large dollop of shaving cream into a resealable plastic bag. Add drops of food coloring in two different primary colors to the bag. Close the bag, removing as much air as possible. Encourage a child to squeeze the bag until a new color appears. It's magic!

Joyce Anderson—Four-Year-Olds
Jewish Community Center Of Greater Minneapolis
Minneapolis, MN

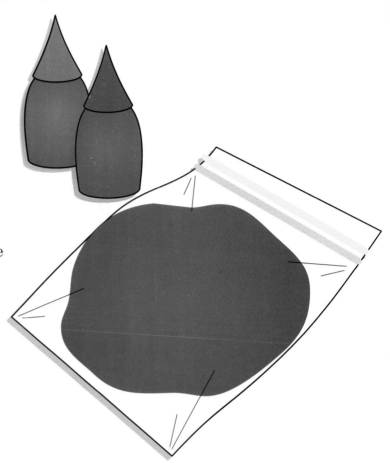

Stir It Up

Stir up color skills with a collection of paint-stirring sticks from local paint stores. Paint the end of each stick a different color. (If you have enough sticks, paint several sticks of each color.) Store all of the sticks in a paint can. For each color of stick, wrap a matching color of construction paper around a can. (Depending on your youngsters' skill levels, you might only label each of the cans with a color word.) Have a youngster match colors by putting each paint stick in the appropriate can.

Karen D. Turner—Gr. K
Red Boiling Springs School
Red Boiling Springs, TN

red

Scoop The Balls!

Your youngsters will have fun separating balls by color at this fun-filled center. Pour several inches of water in a water table. Place a quantity of different-colored Ping-Pong® balls in the water. Station a fishnet and a bucket nearby. Using one hand, a child manipulates the fishnet to scoop the balls, then drops the balls into the bucket. Have him do the activity again, using his other hand. If desired, also have the youngster count the number in each group.

Terry Price—Gr. K
Parkview Elementary
Richmond, IN

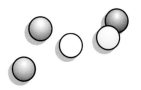

Colorful Class Mascot

Help little ones learn their colors by focusing on one color each month. Designate days for children to wear clothing of that month's color. If you have a class mascot such as a stuffed toy or puppet, purchase a child's size small shirt in each of the colors that will be a monthly focus. Using fabric paint, decorate the shirts with the mascot's name or with holiday symbols. Youngsters will love to see even their mascot dressed to impress.

Debra Rupp—Four-Year-Olds
Kid's World Learning Center
Delta, OH

Rainbow Week

Try these ideas for a colorful week of activities that will result in a rainbow of learning. Bring a large box to circle time. On Monday, have students help you paint one side of the box red. Discuss items that can be red; then have each child find something in the room that is red and bring it back to the circle. Ask each child to tell what he found; then have him put his red item in the box. Continue in this manner through the week, painting a different side of the box each day: blue on Tuesday, yellow on Wednesday, and green on Thursday. On Friday, paint the bottom of the box all the colors of the rainbow. Explain that when you mix together the other colors on the box (red, blue, and yellow), you can make the remaining colors of the rainbow. Ask each child to find something in the room that has a rainbow of colors on it. To add to the fun of Rainbow Week, ask your youngsters to wear clothing in the color designated for each day. On Friday, wear a rainbow of colors.

Donna Osborne—4- and 5-year-olds
Ruggles Street Learning Center
Greensboro, NC

Color Catch

Youngsters will have a ball as they play this color-recognition game. Use assorted colors of construction paper to create one headband for each child to wear. After seating the children in a circle, assist each player in identifying the color of the headband he is wearing by giving directions such as: "All greens, stand up," or "All reds, clap." Next hand a small ball to one child and give him a specific direction based on the color of the headband he is wearing. For example you might say, "Orange, roll the ball to someone wearing a red head-band." Then, "Red, roll the ball to someone wearing a blue headband." Play until each child has had a chance to participate in the fun.

Sr. M. Henrietta—Grs. Pre/K and K
Villa Sacred Heart
Danville, PA

Color Chain

Make a giant color chain as you study colors through the year. When focusing on each color, make a paper chain using construction-paper strips of that color. Use at least as many links as there are children plus a few extras. Hang the completed chain on a wall or from your ceiling. Each time you make a chain, connect it to the previously made color chain(s). Soon a colorful chain will wrap around your whole room! Leave it up until you teach a rainbow, weather, or spring unit. At that time, take the chain down and separate the links. Give a link of every color to each child. Assist him in putting his links together to make his very own rainbow chain. Watch the chain reaction of smiles!

Mary Schroeder—Three- And Four-Year-Olds
Mt. Zion Lutheran Preschool
Greenfield, WI

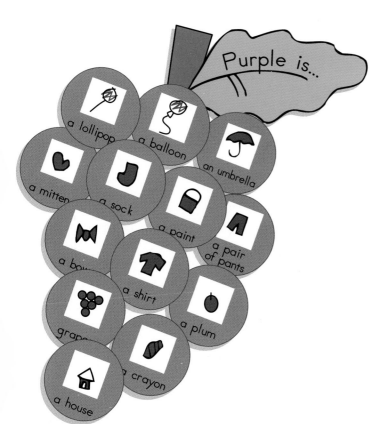

Purple Is...

Your bunch will enjoy learning about the color purple with this grape idea. Provide each child with a small square of white paper and a purple crayon. Ask him to draw and color a picture of something that could be purple. On a purple circle that is somewhat larger than the square, have him write (or dictate for you to write) the name of the object. Glue the squares onto the purple circles; then glue the circles together to resemble a bunch of grapes. Add stem and leaf cutouts; then write, "Purple is...." Snack on real purple grapes when your project is complete.

Marie Stoner
Gorrell Elementary School
Massillon, OH

Blue.

Time To Spare?
Here's a colorful idea to help fill those few extra minutes between activities. Call out a color word. Have students walk quickly and place their hands on an item in the classroom that matches the color you called. Continue with other color words to fill the time as needed. On another day, vary the activity by calling out texture words.

Tracey Rebock—Pre-K
Temple Emanuel Preschool
Cherry Hill, NJ

No-stick Quick Color
Add a little zing to macaroni and rice activities by adding color without the sticky mess! When coloring macaroni (or rice), place the macaroni in a large bowl with a few drops of food coloring and a small amount of rubbing alcohol. Stir the macaroni mixture quickly; then pour it onto a tray. This allows the alcohol to evaporate quickly, which will prevent the macaroni from becoming sticky. Color it beautiful!

Emily Porter—Gr. K
Garth Elementary
Georgetown, KY

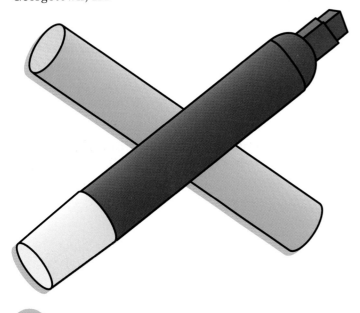

Reinforcing Colors
Use markers and colored chalk to help your students recognize the color of the week. Write on the board with chalk in the special color. Use a marker in the same color to grade students' work. You'll add a little color to your daily routine while you improve your students' recognition of the color of the week.

Margie Cavender—Gr. K
Wilson Elementary School
Crawford, TN

Color Tornadoes

Create a whirlwind during your color unit with this fun activity. Fill a pie pan half full of milk. Have students gently squeeze different-colored drops of food coloring at evenly spaced intervals around the pan. Then pour small amounts of dishwashing liquid in various spots around the side of the pan to break the surface tension and start color tornadoes.

Joyce Montag
Slippery Rock, PA

Alphabet Rainbow

Here's a colorful way to help each child learn the letters in his name and become familiar with alphabetical order at the same time. Print the first six uppercase letters of the alphabet on squares cut from red construction paper. Print the next six letters on orange squares, the next five letters on yellow squares, the next five letters on green squares, and the last four letters on blue squares. (If desired, print the corresponding lowercase letter on the back of each square.) Arrange the letter squares in alphabetical order in five curves to form a rainbow. Select a child to come to the rainbow and find all of the letters in his name. That child then mixes the collected squares and chooses another student to replace them in the rainbow.

Sr. M. Henrietta—Grs. Pre/K and K

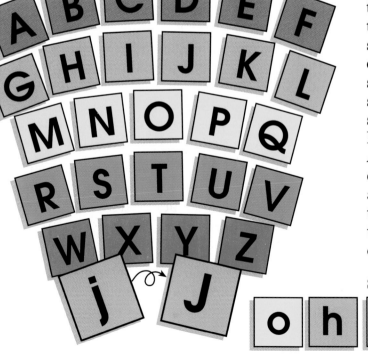

Cool, Color-Changing Drink

Refresh your youngsters with this cool, color-changing drink. In advance prepare blue or red ice cubes and a pitcher of lemonade. Add yellow food coloring to the lemonade to brighten the color if desired. Pour each child a serving of lemonade in a clear plastic cup. Give him a colored ice cube to put in his drink. Have the child stir his drink with a spoon or stirring stick. As he stirs, the blue or red will mix with the yellow to create a color change. Cool!

Mary Johnson—Preschool
Indian Hills Preschool
Gallup, NM

Here A Hand, There A Hand, Here A Foot, There A Foot!

Oh, my! This version of the game Twister® is sure to be a hands-down favorite! To prepare, cut a large rectangle from a white shower-curtain liner. Use a permanent marker to visually divide the rectangle into six sections. Cut hand and foot patterns from heavy paper. Trace the patterns onto the rectangle so that there is a pair of hands and a pair of feet in each section. Using permanent markers, color the hands and feet in each section the same primary color—using the same color in the two sections in each column. Use the patterns to cut as many hands and feet from red, blue, and yellow construction paper as there are on the gameboard. Store the cutouts in a bag.

To play the game with a small group of children, first request that the children remove their shoes so that little fingers and toes will not be hurt if stepped on. Select a cutout from the bag. Have a volunteer place the corresponding body part on the matching section of the gameboard. Play until each child in the group has had several turns.

Grace Daniels—5- To 11-Year-Olds, Multiply Disabled
Winfield Street Elementary School
Corning, NY

Our Favorite Skittles

7	6	3	4

Skittles® Graphing

Here's a rainbow of graphing fun. In advance, prepare a bag for each child that contains a Skittles® candy of each color. Then cut a supply of construction paper circles in matching colors. Have youngsters sample each color of candy with you, then name things that are the same color. After all colors of candy have been sampled, have each youngster personalize a circle to match his color (or taste) preference and attach it to a class graph titled "Our Favorite Skittles."

Tanya Wheeler—Gr. K
Pelahatchie Elementary
Pelahatchie, MS

Color Detectives

Youngsters unlock the secrets of colors when they become color detectives. Label the tab of a folder with a color word. Discuss the word with your youngsters, and have them glue matching paper inside the folder. Give each youngster a personalized Ziploc® bag. Ask him to fill with small items of the featured color and place it inside the folder. If his findings are accurate, he's ready to move on to a new color investigation.

Nina Tabanian—Pre/K
St. Bernard Of Clairvaux
Dallas, TX

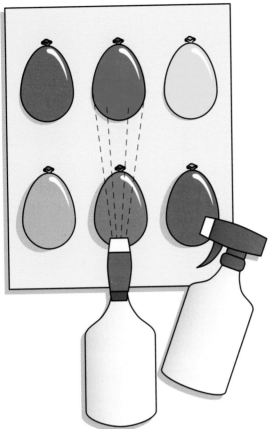

Give It A Squirt!

Is it a warm and sunny day? Take this game out for some water play! To prepare the game, you will need six different-colored balloons, six tacks, a large piece of cardboard, and a squirt bottle full of water. Inflate each balloon, knot it, and tack it to the cardboard. Prop the cardboard against a wall outside. To play, a child stands in front of the board and holds the squirt bottle. Depending on the child's ability, state a series of one, two, or three directions. For example to reinforce colors, you might say, "Squirt the blue balloon, then the yellow balloon, then the red balloon." To reinforce counting, you might say, "Squirt the green balloon three times." Go ahead—give it a squirt!

Rachel Meseke Castro
Juneau Elementary
Juneau, WI

Star-Spangled Bottles

Add some colorful sparkle to your classroom with these star-spangled bottles. To make one star-spangled bottle, remove the label from a clean, clear 16-ounce plastic soda bottle. Pour at least 1/2 cup of light corn syrup into the bottle. Then add a few drops of food coloring and some star-shaped foil confetti. Hot-glue the lid onto the bottle. Label the bottle with the color of its syrup. Encourage children to comment on the movement of the liquid and stars as they shake, turn, and rotate the bottle.

Terri Gulla—Three-Year-Olds
Cutler Ridge United Methodist
    Kindergarten
Miami, FL

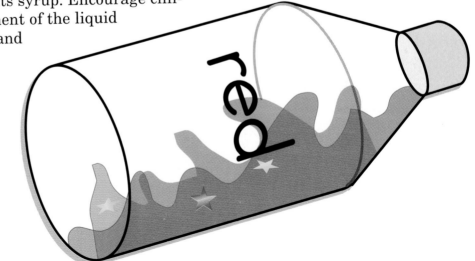

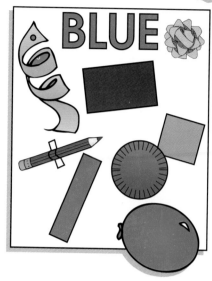

Keep these colorful collages on display to brighten any rainy day! Each time you focus on a color, invite youngsters to bring small, disposable items of that color from home. Label a piece of poster board with the color word; then mount the objects on the board. Make a collage for each color you study; then create a rainbow of color in your room by displaying the collages together at students' eye level.

Laurie Bachmann—Three-Year-Olds, Messiah Lutheran Child Care Center, Park Ridge, IL

Colorful Movement

Looking for a fun way to reinforce color recognition, develop thinking skills, and promote fitness? If so, try this colorful movement game. Ask each child to find his own space in an open area. Depending on children's interest levels and abilities, announce movement directions such as, "If you are wearing blue, hop on one foot," or "If you are *not* wearing yellow, shake your arms." Be sure to adapt your directions to match students' physical abilities as well. Get moving!

Linda Anne Lopienski
Asheboro, NC

Color Game

Give each child a red, green, blue, or yellow child-shaped cutout. Encourage her to move her color fellow at the appropriate time.

Red, green, blue, and yellow:
These are the color fellows.
Hold yours up when you hear its name.
It's time to play a color game.

Red, Red, move so high.
Reach and try to touch the sky.

Green, Green, move round and round.
Circle up and circle down.

Blue, Blue, move left and right.
Move until you're out of sight.

Yellow, Yellow, move front and back.
Keep on moving. Stay on track.

Our color game is almost done.
Let's play again; oh what fun!

— adapted from a poem by Michelle Johnson and
René Jenkins, Lakeland, FL

Reproducible Activities...

Color Fun In The Sun

Read.

Color.

Cut on the solid lines.

Staple.

Color
Fun
In The
Sun

green

brown

blue

orange

red

yellow

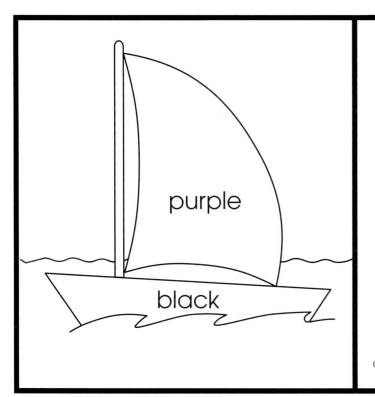

This is my favorite color.

Award

Hurray!

_____
(name)

can read these color words!

☀ yellow		red ☀	
☀ black		green ☀	
☀ purple		orange ☀	
☀ blue		brown ☀	

_____
(teacher's signature)

Name _____

A Sack Of Sweets

Read.

Color.

green

yellow

black

blue

orange

red

brown

purple

Name _____

Hooray for Hats

Read.  Color.

brown

blue

yellow

black

green

purple

orange

red

Name _____

Creamy Construction

🖍 Color.

(46)

red

orange

yellow

brown

black

green

purple

blue

Super Scoops

✏️ Print the missing letters.

🖍️ Color.

yellow

ye _ _ o _

_ _ _ _ ll _ _

blue

_ l _ e

green

g _ e _ n

g _ e _ _

red

_ e _

©The Education Center, Inc. • *Colors* • Preschool/Kindergarten • TEC3172

Singing In The Rain

Look at the color words.

Color each ☂ .

yellow

brown

orange

black

green

purple

gray

red

blue